The Pet Plan and Pet Trust Guide

Dedicated to and created with love on behalf of our pet companions
who faithfully and lovingly serve us and who depend on we human beings for protection.

Copyright ©2008 All rights reserved.
Published by Faux Paw Media Group, A Division of Faux Paw Productions, Inc.™

No part of this book may be reproduced or transmitted in any form or by any means electronic, mechanical, including photocopying, recording or by any information storage and retrieval system without express written permission in writing from the author.

Cataloging-in-publishing data
Colgate, Kimberly Adams

Illustrated by Debby Carman

Summary: Illustrated guide detailing how to prepare, plan and establish
an actual legal trust for pets long term security and protection

ISBN #978-0-9777340-9-2

Create A Pet Trust LLC and Faux Paw Productions is committed to bringing jobs back to America!
We want to make sure your pets are safe!

This book is written and printed in Sarasota, Florida, in the United States of America!
Help us help America!

The Pet Plan and Pet Trust Guide

Our pets trust us to take care of them

A guide to setting up a Pet Plan and a Pet Trust
if you are gone for a day, a week or forever!

Your Guide includes a fill-in-the-blank Pet Trust Form!

Written by **Kimberly Adams Colgate**
Author of "The Everything Wills & Estate Planning Book"
Illustrated by: Debby Carman

Author's Forward

As an attorney, a former full-time law professor and author of the **Everything Wills & Estate Planning Book,** I have spent my career helping families plan for the future.

In my law practice I discovered that most of my clients consider their pets as members of their family. Pets are an intrinsic part of their personal lives and lifestyles and are regarded, in many instances, like their own children. Pets are referred to as best friends, companions, and provide their owners with a continual source of wonder, amusement, comfort and fulfillment. The loyalty and devotion my clients share with their pets brings them their greatest source of joy and entertainment.

The Pet Plan and Pet Trust Guide gently guides the pet owner through each step necessary to create and document a step-by-step emergency pet plan. The Pet Plan and Pet Trust Guide explains what kind of legal documents are available to protect your pets. Drawing from my professional experience as an attorney and former law professor, I thoroughly present and explain the advantages and disadvantages of each type of legal document. My objective is to teach you, the pet owner, how to create and fund a pet trust under the new pet trust laws.

As a pet owner, you don't have to hire a lawyer to learn the rules and create a legally binding pet trust document. As an estate planning attorney with 30 years of experience and the author of the well known Everything Wills & Estate Planning Book, I have created the Pet Plan and Pet Trust Guide to save pet owners hundreds and sometimes thousands of dollars.

Playful, whimsical illustrations were designed by renown artist Debby Carman to enchant you while you learn how to create a pet plan and pet trust.

The Pet Plan and Pet Trust Guide presents a clear legal road map on how to create a pet trust and provides you with a fill-in-the-blank, legally binding pet trust document form.

Don't leave your pet without a plan!

Kimberly A. Colgate, J.D., LL.M
Attorney At Law
Masters In Taxation

Table of Contents

Chapter One
About Your Pet

Your pets are helpless. They depend on you for everything. If you are gone for a day, a week or forever, your pets need a plan.

The Pet Plan and Pet Trust Guide helps you create an emergency plan which will protect your pet.

The first step in your emergency pet plan is to gather and document all of the important information about your pet in one place. If an emergency happens, and you are unexpectedly unavailable, The Pet Plan and Pet Trust Guide will provide all of the information anyone would need to take care of your pet until you come home. And, writing this information in your book will also help you get ready to create a long-term plan for your pet.

The first step in your Pet Plan is to provide all of the important information about your pet.

Let's get started gathering the information about your pet.

IDENTIFY YOURSELF:

Pet Owner's Name:

_____

_____

Pet Owner's Address:

_____

_____

Pet Owner's Telephone Number(s):
Home _____

Work _____

Cell _____

FAX _____

More about me!

INFORMATION ABOUT YOUR PET

Your pet's name:

_____

Your pet's full legal name.

_____

Does your pet have a microchip, or some other form of identification?
Yes _____ or No _____

If Yes, please insert the microchip or other identifying number:

_____

Please insert your pet's Dog License Number & Issuing Agency:
Tag Number: _____
Issued By: _____

If your pet is AKC (American Kennel Club) registered, please provide your pet's AKC registration number.

Your pet's date of birth:

Place Pet
Picture Here

EMERGENCY CONTACT INFORMATION

Name_____

Address_____

City/State/Zip_____

Home Telephone_____

Cell Phone_____

FAX_____

Work Phone_____

Veterinarian phone_____

Nearest relative name and phone_____

Nearest neighbor name and phone_____

Local Police_____

Sometimes it's important to have more than one emergency contact!
[Insert name, address & telephone number of alternative contact]

Name _____

Address _____

_____

Phone Number_____

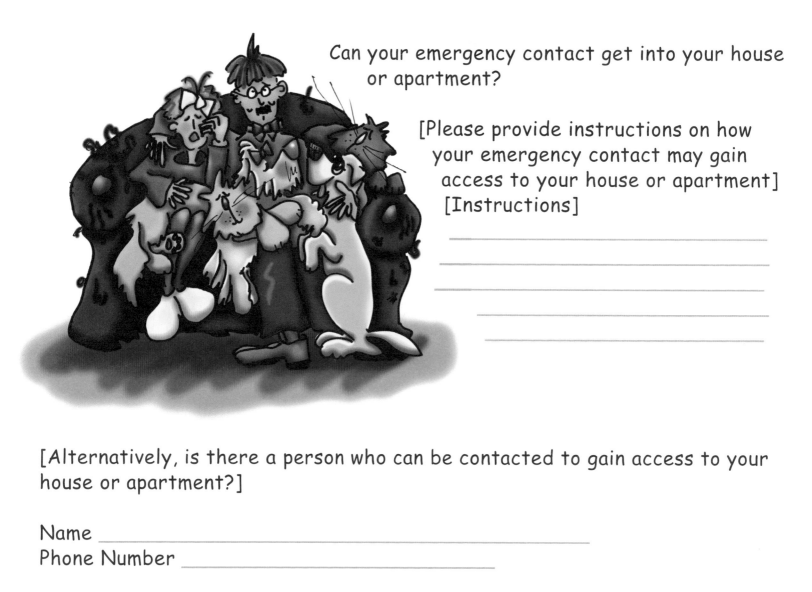

Can your emergency contact get into your house or apartment?

[Please provide instructions on how your emergency contact may gain access to your house or apartment] [Instructions]

_____

_____

_____

_____

_____

[Alternatively, is there a person who can be contacted to gain access to your house or apartment?]

Name _____

Phone Number _____

MEDICAL INFORMATION ABOUT YOUR PET

Vet Name _____

Vet Address _____

_____

Vet Phone Number
_____

24 Hour Emergency Vet Clinic Phone
_____

What was the date of your pet's last vaccines?

Rabies [Insert date] _____
Fleas   [Insert date] _____
_____ [Insert date] _____
_____ [Describe & insert date] _____

_____

_____

Does your pet take any medications? Yes _____ or No _____
If Yes, please describe the medication and dosage:
[Don't forget about the flea medication and the Heart Guard!]

_____

_____

Where do you keep your pet's medications?
[Describe where the medications can be found]

_____

_____

Does your pet have any other medical problems?
[Please describe]

_____

_____

_____

_____

_____

_____

Has your pet been neutered? Yes _____ or NO _____

YOUR PET'S EATING HABITS

What kind of food does your pet eat? [Insert brand]

_____

Where do you keep
your pet food? Special
spot?

_____

Does the pet have any
medication taken with meals?

_____

Do you add "people" food
to your pet's food?
Yes _____ or No _____

[Describe how you
prepare your pet's food]

_____

_____

How often do you feed your pet?

_____

Does your pet eat at a particular time?
[Insert time(s)] _____

How much [Insert amount] do you
feed your pet at each meal?

_____

_____

Do you give your pet treats between
meals? [Please describe treats]

_____

_____

_____

YOUR PET'S SLEEPING HABITS -- Where does your pet sleep?

In bed with you? _____

In a crate? _____

In a special bed? _____

In a cage? _____

Other?
[Please describe where your pet sleeps]

_____

_____

_____

_____

_____

_____

YOUR PET'S POTTY HABITS

Do you take your pet
outside to go to potty?
Yes _____ No _____

Do you use a special leash?
Yes _____ No _____

Does your pet wear a collar
or a harness? (circle one)

Where is the leash, collar or harness located? Does the collar have ID tags on
it? If so, what information is on that tag?

_____

Please describe the walking leash.

_____

How frequently do you take your pet out?

_____

[Insert any special walking instructions]

_____

WHERE DOES YOUR PET STAY WHEN YOU ARE AWAY?

Has your pet ever been left overnight at a kennel?
Yes _____ or No _____

[Please provide the name, address & telephone number of your pet's kennel or boarding facility]

Name _____

Address _____

_____

Phone _____

We're coziest in our own bed!

Circle the items that best describe your pet:

 Frightened by sudden noise, such as fire trucks, sirens, skateboards, honking horns.

 Escape artist - will run away or bolt if given the opportunity.

 Obeys on command.

 Knows his or her name when spoken.

 Rides well in a car.

 Is accustomed to being transported in a pet carrier.

Walks well on a leash / standard collar / choke collar / body harness (circle applicable choice).

 Wears a 'no bark' collar.

 Is fully potty trained.

 Known or prone to have "potty accidents in the home."

Any quirks or peculiarities? (describe)

_____

_____

_____

_____

_____

_____

Is your pet afraid of being left at a kennel?

Yes _____ or No _____

Are there any instructions you can provide that
will help ease your pet's anxiety?

_____

_____

_____

_____

COUTURE AND GROOMING

Does your pet wear any special clothing?

Does your pet wear a collar,
a harness or a muzzle when he /
she goes out?

What about grooming? Anyone in a care giving position will need to know
about BRUSHING, COMBING, BATHING (the fluff parlor phone number or
groomer details) as well as hair clips, hair bows or other accoutrements
needed to keep hair out of face or mouth, or ears out of food etc.?

YOUR PET'S PLAYTIME

Does your pet have special toys?
[Please describe the toys your pet likes most]

Please describe any other information your emergency contact needs to know about your pet.

Chapter Two

THE EMERGENCY PET PLAN

Now that you've completed Chapter One, you have begun to prepare for that rainy day.

STEP ONE OF YOUR EMERGENCY PET PLAN:
The first step of your emergency pet plan is to contact your emergency pet sitters. Find out if they are willing to implement an emergency plan for your pet(s).

You absolutely need someone who can care for your pets on an emergency basis. You never know what can happen!

You may be delayed due to an illness in your family; you may experience travel delays; or, there may be a medical emergency, which may detain you for hours, or even days!

Here's that rainy day

Talk to your emergency pet sitter about what would happen if it were several hours, days, weeks, or, the unthinkable, forever.

The information in Chapter One will make it much easier for your emergency pet sitter.

It is important that you and your pet sitter agree on an emergency plan.

 Will your pet stay at your pet sitter's home?

 Will your pet sitter stay at your house?

 Will your pet sitter make arrangements to board your pet?

Let your pet sitter know where to find your Pet Plan and Pet Trust Guide Book.

STEP TWO OF YOUR EMERGENCY PET PLAN

GIVE YOUR EMERGENCY CONTACT ACCESS TO YOUR HOME

Make sure your pet sitter has access to your home. Your pet sitter, when contacted, needs to be able to get into your house or apartment.

TELL YOUR PET SITTER WHERE TO LOCATE THIS BOOK!

Leave your Pet Plan and Pet Trust Guide Book prominently displayed in your home.

Why? When there is an emergency, it is quite likely that someone other than your emergency pet sitter will go to your home. They will find your pets at home alone. That person may or may not know about your emergency pet plan.

How will he or she know what to do?

When he or she finds your Pet Plan and Pet Trust Guide Book, he or she will know what to do to help your pets.

STEP THREE OF YOUR EMERGENCY PET PLAN.

Your "The Pet Plan and Pet Trust Guide" Book contains an emergency card. You should fill out the card, and place it in your wallet behind your driver's license.

It lets emergency personnel (police, fire or other rescue worker) know that you have a pet or pets at home and lets the emergency personnel know how to contact your pet sitter.

The actual card to fill out is contained in the back of the The Pet Plan and Pet Trust Guide Book.

In Case of Emergency

The holder of this card has a PET at home that will need attending to in the event of an emergency.

Pet Owner(s) Name _____

Pet Owner(s) Address _____

_____

Pet Owner(s) Home Phone Number _____

My Pet will need Attention. Please call my designated pet caregiver at

_____

Caregiver's Name _____

The Pet Plan and Pet Trust Guide

Pet Identification Card

Pet's Name _____ Male ___ Female ___

Breed _____ Birthdate or Age _____

Color _____ Weight _____

Pet License # _____ Microchip # _____

All details concerning this pet can be located in My "Pet Plan and Pet Trust Guide" Book located at _____

_____

Congratulations!

I'm so glad you made a plan for us!

You have just finished compiling all of the necessary information your pet will need in the event of an emergency.

Now you are ready to prepare a long-term plan for your pet.

Chapter Three

WHAT KIND OF LEGAL DOCUMENTS

WOULD PROTECT MY PETS?

Before you can create a long-term plan for your pet, you need to understand what types of documents and legal arrangements are available.

Some documents are easier to create, but are more expensive for your loved ones after you are gone.

Other documents are more challenging to create now, but will save your loved ones a substantial amount of money after you are gone.

And yet other documents just won't work to protect your pets after you are gone.

LET'S GET STARTED!
There are 3 ways you can provide for your pet after you are gone

1. A Will

2. A Trust

3. An Agreement

Each of these documents or legal arrangements have advantages and disadvantages.

CAN I PROVIDE FOR MY PET IN MY WILL?

The answer is yes and no.

You **can not** leave property directly to your pet in your Will because your pet is not a person. But, you can leave property to a person in your Will who is charged with the responsibility of caring for your pet after you are gone. What you are really doing when you choose to provide for your pet in your Will, is, you are creating a trust inside of your Will for your pet - this is commonly known as a **testamentary trust**.

Read on!

You are going to learn all about pet Wills & Trusts.

The main advantage to providing for your pet in your Will is the cost-efficiency associated with creating the Will.

A Will is the easiest and most economical document to create to provide for your pet.

You're going to find saving a dollar now will cost more later. But, after you are gone, providing for your pet in your Will can be hazardous to your pet's health.

WHY DOESN'T A WILL PROTECT MY PETS?

Most people don't understand how a Will works.

The instructions you put in your Will are not carried out automatically. When you are gone there is a lengthy and formal process that must be followed in each state to probate a Will.

The term "to probate a Will" means to establish the legal validity of a Will.

If you provide for your pet in your Will, some-one must petition the probate court to be appointed executor (sometimes known as a personal representative) of your Will.

32

It is almost impossible to initiate the probate process without hiring a lawyer because there are detailed court rules and forms required to probate a Will.

By the time your family makes an appointment with a lawyer, your lawyer prepares the papers to open your estate and initiate the probate of your Will, and the local probate judge signs an order admitting your Will to probate and appoints an executor or personal representative, several weeks, and sometimes several months have elapsed.

Where are your pets for weeks or months?

Who is caring for your pet while this is going on?

Not only is there a big delay before your Will is admitted to probate, there is a substantial cost associated with the probate process.

PROVIDING FOR YOUR PET IN YOUR WILL IS NOT THE BEST RECOMMENDATION. BUT A PLAN FOR YOUR PET CONTAINED IN YOUR WILL IS BETTER THAN NO PLAN AT ALL.

Chapter Four describes how to provide for your pet in your Will.

I'm sorry about the delay in picking you up. It took the Judge longer than I expected to start the probate process.

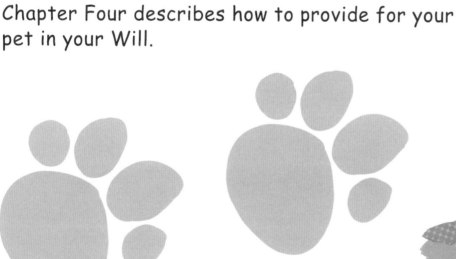

CONSIDER THE ADVANTAGES OF A PET TRUST

Why would you create a Pet Trust to provide for your pet?

There are many advantages to providing for your pet by creating a Pet Trust.

🐾 First, the money needed to care for your pet is immediately available when you create a Pet Trust for the care of your pet.

Second, creating a Pet Trust for your pet allows you to establish a management plan for the care of your pet. The assets you set-aside in your Pet Trust will be distributed for the benefit of your pet according to the instructions you include in your Pet Trust document.

Third, your Pet Trust will provide a method for assuring that your pet is receiving the care described in your Pet Trust document.

It is not expensive to create a Pet Trust for your pet.
You don't need to be rich to fund the trust.

Read on!

 Chapter Four - will tell you all about Wills.

 Chapter Five - will teach you all about how to create your Pet Trust.

 Chapter Nine - contains an actual pet trust document.

CAN'T I JUST HAVE AN AGREEMENT?

Most people feel they have adequately provided for their pet by making arrangements (usually a verbal agreement) with a family member or friend to take their pet when they are gone. There are countless reasons why this type of agreement does not provide the security your pet needs.

🐾 First, who enforces the verbal agreement to make sure your pet is cared for?

🐾 Second, did the person with whom you had an agreement really understand what you wanted?

Please don't rely on a verbal agreement to take care of me!

Third, will your family argue? Will your family give the caregiver, the person with whom you had a verbal agreement, the money to take care of your pet?

The first and foremost is that no one loves your pet the way you do. Pets are very devoted to their owners. When tragedy strikes, your family is typically not focused on the well being of your pet. Your family is dealing with their own emotional loss, and frankly, might not understand your devotion to your pet. And, keep in mind your pet will grieve your loss.

Think about the simple logistics -
IF YOU ARE GONE

Who will take your pet within 24 hours of your passing?

42

Where will your pet stay?

 What will your pet eat?

 Where will your pet sleep?

 Who will pay for all of this?

 Your pet may be grieving that you are gone.

 Will your pet be boarded while your family makes arrangements for you?

 Your pet will not understand.

 Your pet will be waiting and waiting and waiting for you!

If you have a well-drafted Pet Trust, all of these contingencies can be addressed, planned and provided for.

A verbal agreement usually does not work!

43

Chapter Four
PROVIDING FOR YOUR PET IN YOUR WILL

Before you decide to provide for your pet in your Will, you need to understand what a Will is, and how it will operate.

WHAT IS A WILL?

A Will is a legal document that directs how your property will be distributed when you are gone.

Your Will names an Executor (in some states known as a Personal Representative) who is legally responsible for paying your taxes and debts and distributing your property according to the instructions contained in your Will.

Before you learn the rules on how to provide for your pet in your Will, you need to understand the basics about how a Will is administered.

Many people are under the misunderstanding that if they die and have a Will, that the Executor merely follows the instructions in the Will, and distributes your property.

This could not be more incorrect.

When a person owns property in his or her name when he or she dies, there is a lengthy and very formal process that must be followed in each state to administer your Will.

The typical steps that must be followed to administer your Will are:

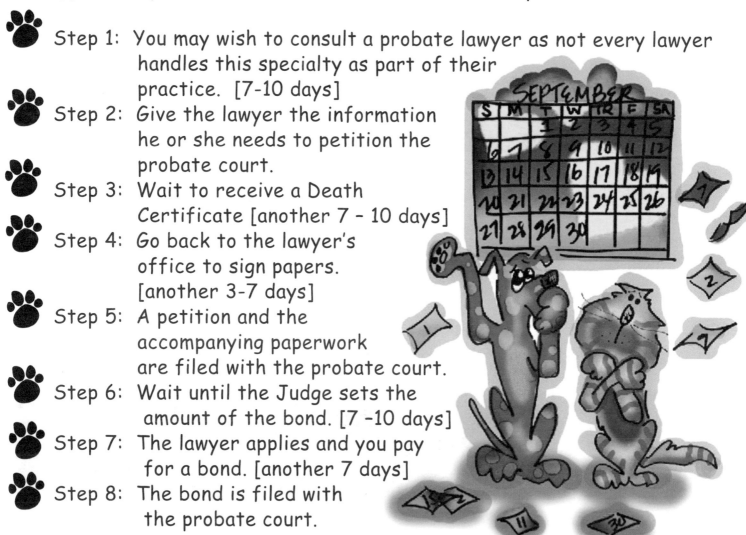

Step 1: You may wish to consult a probate lawyer as not every lawyer handles this specialty as part of their practice. [7-10 days]

Step 2: Give the lawyer the information he or she needs to petition the probate court.

Step 3: Wait to receive a Death Certificate [another 7 – 10 days]

Step 4: Go back to the lawyer's office to sign papers. [another 3-7 days]

Step 5: A petition and the accompanying paperwork are filed with the probate court.

Step 6: Wait until the Judge sets the amount of the bond. [7 –10 days]

Step 7: The lawyer applies and you pay for a bond. [another 7 days]

Step 8: The bond is filed with the probate court.

Step 9: The Judge issues an Order appointing the Executor you name in your Will. [typically 7-10 days]

FINALLY, the Executor is appointed [typical time frame – at least 30 days]

 Step 10: The Executor can now access your money.

BUT, an Executor cannot distribute money unless the Executor is sure there will be sufficient funds to pay all bills - otherwise, the Executor can be personally liable.

 Step 11: The lawyer posts for creditors in local newspaper.

 Step 12: Executor must often wait 3-4 months before he or she can distribute estate funds.

Thank goodness we're not going to be on our own.

48

WHERE ARE YOUR PETS?

If you choose to use a Will as the legal document to provide for your pet, you are going to need to make some informal arrangements for the care of you pet until the probate process can be initiated.

HOW DO I PROVIDE FOR MY PET IN MY WILL?

Your pet is your property. Although some types of pets are registered, such as an A.K.C. (American Kennel Club) registered dog, most pets do not bear any indicia of title. Not to be crude, but pets are like most of your household effects. You don't have a "title" for your furniture, your jewelry or your clothes. Likewise, you don't have a title, in most cases, for your pet.

WHERE WILL WE LIVE?

Contrast this with assets like a bank account titled in your individual name, a share of stock, your house or your car. If you die, and there are assets titled in your individual name there must be a person who is legally empowered to convey title to your assets after you are gone. The "person" who has power to convey title to your assets is your Executor.

Even though your pet does not have a title, your Will can name a new owner for your pet.

That provision might read:

I hereby direct my Executor to convey my pet _____(identify the pet) to _____(identify the person).

- OR-

I hereby devise my pet_____(identify the pet) to_____ (identify the person).

There are no legal formalities on how you word the instructions as long as the Executor can identify the property (your pet) and you have sufficiently described the person or organization to receive your pet.

WHAT HAVE YOU REALLY ACCOMPLISHED?

The only goal you have accomplished is to put in writing who is to receive your pet. You have not:

- Provided support for your pet.
- Given any instructions on how to care for your pet.
- Provided a backup if the person you name is not able to take your pet.

When you leave property, which includes your pet, to a person in your Will, the person is free to "disclaim." This means that they can refuse to take your pet.

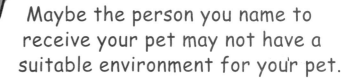

The person you name to receive your pet may really want to take your pet. But, maybe they can't afford to care for your pet.

Maybe the person you name to receive your pet may not have a suitable environment for your pet.

There could be many different reasons why the person you name is unable to take your pet.

THE ONLY GOAL YOU HAVE ACCOMPLISHED IS TO NAME A PERSON WHO MAY OR MAY NOT TAKE YOUR PET!

CAN YOU LEAVE MONEY DIRECTLY TO YOUR PET IN YOUR WILL?

The answer is NO. Your pet is not a person.

Please don't tell your pet this awful reality. Many of us treat our pets like people.

But unfortunately, the law does not treat your pet as a person, and therefore you cannot leave money directly to your pet in your Will.

CAN YOU LEAVE MONEY TO A PERSON NAMED IN YOUR WILL WHO CAN SPEND THE MONEY TO TAKE CARE OF YOUR PET?

The answer is YES and NO.

If you leave money (or property) to a person and state in your Will that you **want them** to spend the money to care for your pet, this is called **precatory language**. In English, it **is merely a wish, and is not enforceable**. It is like leaving money to a person and stating in the Will that you hope they will use the money to buy a new car. The Probate Process has no way of policing to make sure the funds are in fact used to buy a car, or in our case to care for your pet.

CAN YOUR WILL LEAVE PROPERTY TO A PERSON WHO MUST SPEND THOSE FUNDS TO CARE FOR YOUR PET?

The answer is Yes. You can create a Pet Trust inside of your Will for the care of your pet. This is called a Testamentary Trust. What you are really doing is creating a trust for your pet, and the terms of the Pet Trust happened to be set out in the Will.

I do not recommend a Testamentary Trust inside your Will.

WHY?

 First, there are all of those delays and costs associated with the probate process.

 Second, the provisions for your pet get all mixed up with the distribution of your other property.

Third, while your heirs bicker over your property, there is no plan in place for your pet.

Who could love us as much as you?

CONCLUSION.

You could name a person who is to "inherit" your pet in your Will. You could leave money to that person, with the hope they will spend the money to defray the cost of caring for your pet, **BUT THIS ARRANGEMENT IS NOT ENFORCEABLE!**

If you are going to just name a person to receive your pet in your Will, you might as well just have a verbal agreement or write the intended caregiver a nice note.

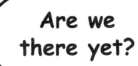

Chapter Five

WHAT IS A REVOCABLE PET TRUST AND HOW DO I CREATE ONE FOR MY PET?

IS THERE MORE THAN ONE TYPE OF TRUST?

There are two types of trusts. There is a trust you create while you are living, called a Revocable Trust and there is a trust you include in your Will, called a Testamentary Trust. You could create an Irrevocable Trust for your pet or pets while you are living, but this would be very rare. Therefore I have not included information in this book about an Irrevocable Trust.

As you can see from Chapter Four, I do not recommend creating a Testamentary Trust for your pet. A Testamentary Trust, which is included in your Will, cannot take care of your pet until the lengthy and costly probate process occurs. Alternatively, a Revocable Trust's assets are immediately available for the care of your pet when something happens to you.

WHAT IS A REVOCABLE TRUST?

A Revocable Trust for your pet or pets is a legally enforceable document involving five parties:

 The Creator

 The Trustee

 A Successor Trustee

 Beneficiaries

 A Physical Caregiver or Caregivers

You could create one Revocable Trust that would provide for the distribution of all of your property for the benefit of your family, your loved ones and your pet or pets. That trust could leave some property for the care of your pet and the rest of your property for your family and loved ones. However, because the provisions you are going to make for the protection of your pet have different legal and practical limitations, I strongly suggest that you create a separate Revocable Trust for the benefit of your pet or pets. This book will be limited to teaching you how to create a trust that will protect your pet.

LET'S GET STARTED LEARNING THE RULES!

1. You will be the **creator** of your Pet Trust. You will keep the power to change or revoke your trust as long as you are living. This is why your Pet Trust is called a Revocable Trust.

2. You will be the **first trustee** of the your Pet Trust. And, your Pet Trust document will name a person to serve as **Successor Trustee** after you are gone. You could name a bank to serve as Successor Trustee, but this is cost prohibitive for most people.

3. You will be the **beneficiary** of your Pet Trust while you are living.

4. Your pet or pets will be the beneficiaries of your Pet Trust after you are gone.

🐾 5. Your Pet Trust document will name a physical caregiver for your pet or pets. Your Pet Trust document may name more than one physical caregiver. Your Pet Trust document may also name successor physical caregivers, in the event the first physical caregiver you name is not available.

🐾 6. Your Pet Trust will name a beneficiary or beneficiaries who will receive the remaining trust property after your pets or pets are gone.

I don't recommend that you make the Successor Trustee and the physical caregiver the same person. The Successor Trustee should be the person who doles out the money, according to the instructions you have included in your Revocable Pet Trust. The Successor Trustee will make sure that the physical caregiver is doing his or her job.

The Creator.

You will be the creator of your Pet Trust. As the creator of your Pet Trust, you will make all of the decisions, which will be included in your Revocable Pet Trust document.

You, as the Creator of the Pet Trust, will decide:

🐾 Who will actually keep your pet or pets after you are gone? This person will be known as the **physical caregiver**.

🐾 What property will be owned by your Successor Trustee, after you are gone, to provide for the care of your pet or pets?

🐾 Who will manage the property for the care of your pet? This will be the **Successor Trustee**.

🐾 How will the property owned by the trust actually be spent for the benefit of your pet or pets after you are gone? **This will be your pet instructions**.

🐾 What will happen to the trust property in the Pet Trust after your pet or pets are gone?

The Trustee

When you create a Revocable Trust for your pet or pets, you need to name a **trustee**. You will name yourself as the **initial trustee** of your Revocable Pet Trust. There must be an **initial trustee** who owns the property you are transferring to the Pet Trust. You could name someone else as the **initial trustee**, or you could name a **professional trustee**, like a bank, to serve as the **initial trustee**, but most people name themselves as the **initial trustee**. Your Revocable Pet Trust will also name a **Successor Trustee**. The person you name as the **Successor Trustee** is a very important decision.

There are so many decisions to make. I'm sure glad the Pet Trust Book will guide me through this process!

The **Successor Trustee** is the person who will serve as trustee after you are gone.

You might say, "You can stop right there, because I don't want to leave money for my pet until I am gone."

Don't get worried. Remember, you are serving as the **initial trustee**. When you create your Revocable Pet Trust, you are merely transferring money or property from your individual name, into your name as **trustee**. You will continue to have complete control over the money in the Pet Trust while you are alive. It is only after you are gone that the funds in your Pet Trust can be spent for your pet or pets.

Don't get worried about the money, we'll talk more about funding your Revocable Pet Trust later in this book.

WHAT HAPPENS WHEN YOU ARE GONE?

Your Revocable Pet Trust document will name a **Successor Trustee**. When you are gone, the person you name in your Revocable Pet Trust as **Successor Trustee** automatically becomes the new trustee.
It is like the **Successor Trustee** is your **silent partner**.

Your **Successor Trustee** has **no say** in the Pet Trust until you are gone. But your **Successor Trustee** will have immediate access to the money owned by the trust after you are gone.

Your **Successor Trustee** can spend money for the care of your pet **IMMEDIATELY** after you are gone. But, your **Successor Trustee** MUST follow the instructions and directions you, as the creator of the Revocable Pet Trust, include in the trust document.

WHAT ARE THE DUTIES OF YOUR SUCCESSOR TRUSTEE?
Your Revocable Pet Trust becomes irrevocable after you are gone.

Then, your **Successor Trustee** must manage the trust property and spend the trust money for the benefit of your pet or pets.

There are two duties your trustee has regarding the management of the Revocable Pet Trust property.

🐾 The first duty of the **Successor Trustee** is to follow the instructions you have included in the Pet Trust document for the care of your pets.

🐾 The second duty is to manage, invest or safeguard the trust property. I will discuss the second duty in the next chapter about funding your Pet Trust.

After I describe the types of duties a **Successor Trustee** can be given, I am going to provide you with suggestions on how you come up with a plan for your pet or pets.

The plan you develop for your pet or pets will help you develop the instructions and duties you want to include in your Revocable Pet Trust.

WHAT KIND OF INSTRUCTIONS CAN I PUT IN MY REVOCABLE PET TRUST?

THERE ARE TWO TYPES OF INSTRUCTIONS OR DUTIES.

You can give your Successor Trustee either General Instructions and Duties or Specific Instructions or Duties.

WHAT ARE GENERAL INSTRUCTIONS?

General instructions are instructions that give the Successor Trustee the power to exercise his or her discretion or judgment in deciding how much money to spend on your pet or pets and when to spend that money.

For instance, the instructions in your Pet Trust document could state:

"My Successor Trustee shall distribute as much money or property from this Pet Trust to the physical caregiver of my pet or pets as my Successor Trustee feels, in his or her sole discretion, my physical caregiver needs to support and maintain my pet or pets."

When you use a simple general instruction of this nature, you are relying on the Successor Trustee's judgment to spend money for the benefit of your pet, like you would, if you were still living. This places more responsibility on the Successor Trustee you have named in your Pet Trust document.

Please think about the logistics of general instructions.

Remember, the Successor Trustee is typically not the physical caregiver of your pet. Your Successor Trustee will need to distribute or pay money to the physical caregiver of your pet on a regular basis. Therefore, if the instructions in your Pet Trust document merely say:

"Successor Trustee distribute as much money or property as you think my pet or pet needs."

You are leaving it completely up to the Successor Trustee to decide how much and when to distribute money to the physical caregiver for the benefit of your pet or pets. It will probably be a big job and a constant headache to constantly negotiate the amount of money the caregivers feel your pet or pets need.

Specific instructions.

The more time you spend developing a plan for the care of your pet or pets, the less time your Successor Trustee will need to spend.

WHAT ARE SPECIFIC INSTRUCTIONS OR DUTIES?

Specific instructions can be physical or monetary. For instance,

"My Successor Trustee shall pay the physical caregiver of my pet or pets $500 per month."

"My Successor Trustee shall take my pet or pets to the veterinarian at least one time per year."

"My Successor Trustee must pay the caregiver to have his or her backyard fenced."

"My Successor Trustee shall make a physical inspection of the caregiver's home at least once per month."

These are all examples of specific instructions or duties.

In order to provide specific instructions in your Pet Trust document, you are going to need to make a plan and prepare a budget.

PHYSICAL CAREGIVER

Your Revocable Pet Trust should name a physical caregiver for your pet. You need to make sure that the person or persons you are considering are ready, able and willing to take your pet or pets.

You, the Creator of your Revocable Pet Trust, should develop your pet plan before you talk to your perspective physical caregivers. If your caregiver knows what you expect, what duties he or she will have and the proposed financial supplements provided by your Pet Trust document, this may help your perspective physical caregiver decide whether he or she is willing to accept the job, if something should happen to you.

Let's face it - taking care of a pet or pets is a job! Most pet owners don't think about the time they spend on their pets as a job, nor does the pet owner typically calculate how much it costs to support his or her pet.

But, you are going to be asking someone else to be named in your Pet Trust as a physical caregiver. He or she deserves to know the job description, and understand the financial consequences or benefits of assuming that role.

HOW DO I CHOOSE A PHYSICAL CAREGIVER?

I recommend that you follow a process that is very familiar to all of us.

WHO?   WHAT?   WHERE?   WHEN?   AND   WHY?

WHO? --Take separate pieces of paper and write down the name of every person who would be an eligible physical caregiver to take your pet if you are gone. Make sure you put each person's name on a separate piece of paper. You are going to find as we progress through this exercise, you are going to make notes on each piece of paper to help you decide what is best for your pet or pets.

Start with the global approach of **who would love your pet**.

As you progress though this exercise, you may discover that who will love your pet the most is not the most suitable physical caregiver.

WHAT? -- Now, on each eligible candidate's piece of paper, write down what each person has to offer your pet. The factors might include:

 Does your potential caregiver work?

 How often does your pet need to be taken outside?

 Does your potential caregiver(s)' schedule accommodate the care your pet or pets?

 Does your potential caregiver have a spouse?

 Will the caregiver's spouse want your pet living in his or her home?

Who will love us?

Does your potential caregiver have children?

 Are the children old enough to be around your pet?

 Has your pet been around children?

 Does your pet sleep with you?

 Will your pet be able to sleep with your chosen caregiver?

 What do you do with your pet?

 Will your chosen caregiver be able to do what you did for your pet?

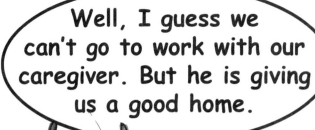

Well, I guess we can't go to work with our caregiver. But he is giving us a good home.

You might want to assign points to these factors. Some factors may be more important to you than others.

WHERE? -- As you analyze each candidate, making notes on their individual pieces of paper, now address the question of where. Think about the following issues:

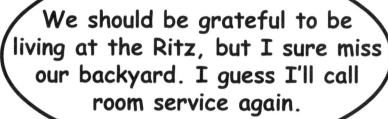

We should be grateful to be living at the Ritz, but I sure miss our backyard. I guess I'll call room service again.

 Where will your pet live?

 Does your potential caregiver own their home? Do they rent?

 If they rent, will the landlord allow your caregiver to have your pet?

 Does your caregiver have enough room for your pet?

Is your pet accustomed to a fenced in yard?

 Does your caregiver have his or her own pets?

 Do you think your pet will adjust to other pets?

No home will be perfect, like yours, but each potential physical caregiver's environment should be evaluated to determine the strengths and weaknesses.

WHEN? -- Would each possible physical caregiver be able to take your pet immediately? Remember, your pet can't pick up the phone and order take-out food. Your pet must be fed, watered, and in the case of a dog, let outside. A cat may be able to survive a bit longer than a dog, but a cat's food and water will only last so long.

As you evaluate each possible physical caregiver, you may determine that your pet's management plan needs an interim or immediate plan for your pet, which is different than the longer-term plan. Your Pet Trust might direct that your pet be boarded temporarily, until the permanent caregiver can make arrangements to take your pet or pets. Alternatively, your plan may contain instructions for a neighbor or friend to care for your pet, until permanent arrangements can be coordinated.

As you proceed through this who, what, where, when and why exercise, you may find yourself eliminating candidates who you previously might have considered as the best physical caregiver for your pet.

WHY? -- After you have made notes on each candidate for physical caregiver's piece of paper, the why may become more self-evident. For example, it may be that the person who would "love" your pet the most, is not the best candidate to serve as the physical caregiver because of one of the other variables or factors noted on his or her sheet.

There's no place like home, but this is as close as it gets!

The more carefully you analyze your possible choices, the more likely it would be that it would be a successful placement if you are gone.

Remember, your Pet Trust is revocable. People often change jobs, move, divorce or they simply can no longer provide for your pet. If circumstances change, you can name an alternate physical caregiver in your Pet Trust. You never want your pet or pets to be without the loving care your pet deserves, merely because circumstances have changed for the original caregiver named.

As you proceed through this book, you may find yourself coming back to the sheets with your candidates' names, and adding more variables to consider.

YOUR PET BUDGET

Many problems can be solved if there is proper funding to care for your pet. You should develop a budget for the care of your pet or pets. Once you have established a budget, you may be able to include specific instructions in your Pet Trust, which will remove some of the discretion or general instructions about how much money your Successor Trustee needs to distribute to the physical caregiver for the care of your pet or pets.

Your pet budget should include the cost of the following items:

🐾 Pet Food

🐾 Pet Toys

🐾 Medical Care

🐾 Grooming

🐾 Housing changes required / Fencing

🐾 Boarding Expenses, in the event your caregiver travels

🐾 Travel Expenses, if your caregiver will take your pet

🐾 Burial or cremation expenses

These expenses are dependent on the age of your dog; and, some expenses just plain cannot be predicted, such as future medical expenses.
Your budget should also take into consideration additional costs associated with the potential lifestyle change of the person you are considering naming as a physical caregiver.

Expenses to get the new home ready. The physical caregiver may need to spend some money to prepare his or her home for your pet or pets. These expenditures might include fencing, a dog or cat house, changes in the floor coverings, pet doors, or other special physical changes to the caregiver's environment.

It is even possible that you want to transfer your home into the Pet Trust and require that your physical caregiver will live in your home as long as your pets are living. But, I would expect most creators of pet trusts will merely be providing trust funds to assist the physical caregiver in preparing his or her home for your pet after you are gone.

It's hard to believe how expensive I am!

Wear and tear expenses. Most pet owners don't calculate the amount they spend cleaning their homes because they are shared with pets. Carpets are cleaned and replaced more often, furniture is soiled and damaged, and bedding is cleaned more often. Remember, more than 10 million pet owners sleep with their pets!

It costs money to maintain the physical environment shared with our pets.

Boarding expenses. As the creator of the Pet Trust you may want to estimate the number of times your physical caregiver will need to board your pets and calculate the annual cost of boarding.

Can you believe how much we cost to maintain?

Medical care. We never know what our pets will need, but, you should be able to calculate the normal life expectancy of your pet and the anticipated annual routine veterinary bills. How much you are able to set aside in your Pet Trust for emergency medical care depends on your financial resources.

Inconvenience or loss of time. It takes time to properly care for a pet. This is very difficult to quantify, but as the creator of the trust you may want to include instructions requiring your Successor Trustee to pay a stipend or a salary to the physical caregiver of your pet or pets. The amount you direct your Successor Trustee to pay your physical caregiver will depend on how much money you have to fund your Pet Trust. Sometimes just a small payment recognizes and compensates the physical caregiver for his or her efforts.

SAMPLE PET BUDGET

Initial expenses:
Dog, cat or pet house: $300.00
Fencing: $2000.00
Interior pet gates: $100.00
Sub-Total: $2,400.00

Monthly expenses:
Pet food: $50 per month
Pet toys: $10 per month
Boarding Expense: $60 per month

Sub-Total: $1,440.00 per year

Annual expenses:
Annual checkups: $150.00
Non-Routine medical: $200.00
                          $350.00

Sub-Total: $350.00 per year

Annual wear and tear: $750.00 per year

Long-term medical:
Estimated cost: $1500.00

TOTAL EXPENSES OVER
10 YEARS = $29,300.00

Expect the unexpected

Without unexpected expenditures, it will cost your physical caregiver $29,300.00 over the lifetime of your pet.

If it costs nothing to set up the caregiver's house to care for your pet, there are no long-term medical costs and there is no annual wear and tear on your caregiver's home, it will still cost $17,940 to care for your pet for 10 years.

$14,440.00 ($1,440 x 10 years) + $3,500.00 ($350.00 x 10 years) = $17,940 to care for your pet for 10 years.

Your trust document should contain specific instructions, such as:

🐾 My Successor Trustee shall distribute $2400 to my pet's physical caregiver to purchase a pet house and install fencing at his or her home.

🐾 My Successor Trustee shall distribute $120 per month to the physical caregiver for pet food, toys and boarding expense.

🐾 My Successor Trustee shall distribute $350 per year for annual check-ups.

🐾 My Successor Trustee shall distribute $750 per year to the physical caregiver for the maintenance and upkeep of my caregiver's home.

The key to providing your pet with proper care is: To have enough money budgeted and funded in your Pet Trust, and to give your Successor Trustee specific distribution instructions.

A COMBINATION OF SPECIFIC AND GENERAL INSTRUCTIONS

Because we don't know what our pet might need, it is a good idea to provide certain specific instructions, such as those outlined above, and include a general provision that the Successor Trustee could expend such amounts of trust funds as the Successor Trustee in his or her sole discretion, feels the pet might need for its maintenance, health and support.

If you don't want to include so many specific instructions, your Pet Trust document could give the Successor Trustee general instructions with a limitation.

You could put in your Pet Trust document that the Successor Trustee is to distribute $300 per month, plus any amount of money he or she feels the pet may need for its health or support. Now you have given your Successor Trustee a specific instruction as well as a general instruction.

The instructions you put in your Pet Trust document will depend on the resources you have available to fund the Pet Trust and how much time you want to devote to planning, calculating and setting out your specific instructions in writing in your trust document.

Chapter 9 includes a fill-in-the-blank pet trust document.

Don't worry! You won't get confused because your fill-in-the-blank pet trust document is carefully keyed. Each blank is numbered. When you check the key included in Chapter 9, it will guide you through how to complete your Pet Trust.

Aaahhhh....
we feel content

Chapter Six

HOW DO I FUND MY TRUST

You have a number of options on how to fund your Pet Trust.

For a revocable trust to be binding, you need to convey at least one dollar from yourself as an individual to yourself as the initial trustee of your Pet Trust.

After you have made a transfer of at least one dollar to yourself as trustee, your Pet Trust is alive and legally enforceable.

$1 won't buy us much food! Will there be money for us after you are gone?

It is very important for you to understand that the very carefully drafted specific and general instructions you put in your Pet Trust for the care of your pet or pets, will not do any good unless there is money or assets in the Pet Trust that can be used for the care of your pet.

If you only transferred one dollar to the Pet Trust and never transferred any additional property, the Successor Trustee whom you have carefully chosen would only have one dollar to spend on the care of your pet.

The best savings are the ones spent to take care of the things we love.

HOW DO YOU GET MONEY OR PROPERTY INTO THE TRUST?

🐾 You either transfer property from your individual name to your name as trustee while you are alive; OR

🐾 You provide a funding mechanism to convey cash or other property to your Pet Trust when you die.

EXAMPLE ONE: MONEY

Let's assume you have a savings account, which normally bears a balance of $10,000. After you have signed your Revocable Pet Trust, all you need to do is go to the local bank where your savings account is located, provide the bank with either a copy of your Revocable Pet Trust, or a Certificate of Trust.

Your bank representative will change the name on your savings account from your name as an individual to your name as trustee of your Revocable Pet Trust.

You will continue to have 100% access to and use of the money in the Pet Trust savings account while you are living. If you are gone, the person you named as Successor Trustee will be the legal owner of the balance in the account.

Your Successor Trustee will have IMMEDIATE ACCESS to the funds. Your Successor Trustee will have money to follow those carefully drafted specific and general instructions you put in your Pet Trust.

Beware, if you spend all of the money in that savings account before you pass away, there will be no funds available for the care of your pet.

You don't have to change the name on an existing account. You could open a new account in your name as Trustee of your Revocable Pet Trust.

You are making **no irrevocable decisions** when you open a new account or you change the name of a financial account from your individual name to your name as trustee of your Pet Trust. **The money is still yours to spend as you see fit.**

When you are gone, the remaining money in that account is in trust for the care of your pet or pets.

EXAMPLE TWO: STOCKS OR INVESTMENT ACCOUNTS

You could transfer other types of property, such as stocks or an investment account.

For example, if you have a stock portfolio, you can make an appointment with your investment advisor or your broker, and you can complete the forms to change the name on your account from your individual name to you name as Trustee of your Revocable Pet Trust.

The process is similar to changing the name on your bank account. You will need to provide your investment advisor or your broker with either a copy of your Revocable Pet Trust, or a Certificate of Trust. Your Investment advisor will prepare the forms to change the name on your account.

You do not have to change the name on your entire investment portfolio. You could open a new account in your name as trustee of your Revocable Pet Trust and transfer just enough stocks or investments into that account to fund you Pet Trust budget.

You will be 100% in charge of your account. When you are gone, your Successor Trustee will become the owner of that investment account for the benefit of your pet or pets, and will be required to spend the money according to the instructions you have put in your Pet Trust.

Your Successor Trustee will have more financial decisions to make if you fund your Pet Trust with stocks or investments. But, if you don't want to burden your Successor Trustee with these types of decisions, your trust document could require that the portfolio be liquidated to cash after your death. Then, your Successor Trustee would have only cash to manage, which could be invested in a liquid mutual fund or savings account.

EXAMPLE THREE: REAL ESTATE

You could even transfer real estate from your name to your name as trustee of your Pet Trust.

If you transfer real estate into your Revocable Pet Trust, your trust document is going to need to provide instructions for what the Successor Trustee is required to do with the real estate after you're gone.

If you are going to fund your Revocable Pet Trust with real estate, I highly recommend that you contact an attorney to assist you with the real estate transfer, and to make sure your Pet Trust is properly funded.

Please drop me, attorney Kimberly A. Colgate, an email at: **kcolgate@FLLAWYER.com** I will direct you to an attorney in your geographic area who can help you with your real estate transfer(s) for the benefit of your pet.

There are so many creative ways you could fund your Pet Trust with real estate. Again, it is important to have an attorney help you with this type of funding. Your trust document would be more complicated, but you could convey your home into your name as trustee of your Pet Trust, and then your document could provide that the physical caregiver should live in your home as long as your pets are living. Oh wow! Talk about a plan.

Notice if you fund your Pet Trust only with real estate, your Successor Trustee will not have any available cash to support your pet, especially if the home will be retained for your pets. If you fund your Pet Trust with real estate, you are going to want to fund the trust with cash or securities to provide liquidity.

If your plan involves funding with real estate, please contact me, attorney Kimberly A. Colgate, at **kcolgate@FLLAWYER.com** to connect you with an attorney who can help you!

EXAMPLE FOUR: LIFE INSURANCE

You could take out a life insurance policy insuring your life, which names your Pet Trust as the beneficiary. This might be an excellent, and cost-efficient way to provide the funding your Pet Trust needs. Unfortunately pets don't live as long as people. If your pet or pets live 15 years, you are really lucky.

This is why term life insurance might be a particularly good option to fund your Pet Trust. Term insurance is typically much cheaper. It is the type of insurance that only lasts the number of years designated by the policy [5 years, 10 years, 15 years, etc]. The policy has no cash value, and only pays a death benefit.

Most persons wishing to provide for the care of their pet are much more likely to fund the Revocable Pet Trust with cash. But, as you can see, your Pet Trust can be funded with any type of property.

All you are doing is changing the owner from yourself as a person, to yourself as trustee. The Successor Trustee you name in your document will automatically become the owner after you are gone, and he or she must manage the property and spend the trust funds according to the specific and general instructions you put in your Pet Trust document for the care of your pet or pets.

Remember, as the creator of the Pet Trust you continue to use, own, manage and spend the property for your benefit while you are alive.

You can change your trust document any time you want.

You can name beneficiaries who will receive the funds remaining in your Pet Trust after your pet or pets are gone.

EXAMPLE FIVE: FUNDING YOUR TRUST THROUGH YOUR WILL

If you don't want to change the name of a financial account from your individual name to your name as trustee; if you don't want to rename or create an investment account in your name as initial trustee; and you don't want to fund with real estate, life insurance or other property, you could leave a bequest in your Will to your Pet Trust.

HOW WOULD YOU DO THIS?
A simple provision in your Will which states:

"I leave $$$$ to [name your Successor Trustee & the name of your Pet Trust].

It's as simple as that. Then the money would flow into your Pet Trust, to be used by the Successor Trustee for the support of your pet or pets.

I DON'T RECOMMEND FUNDING YOUR PET TRUST WITH A BEQUEST FROM YOUR WILL. WHY?

THE MONEY IS NOT AVAILABLE UNTIL THE SLOW, EXPENSIVE, CUMBERSOME PROBATE PROCESS IS WELL UNDER WAY.

But, if you have provided for enough funds for the immediate care of your pet by placing a financial account in your name as trustee, you could provide additional funding for the Pet Trust through your Will.

This option is blending funding a Revocable Pet Trust while you are alive, by naming yourself as trustee, with naming your Pet Trust as an heir under your Will. If you do not have a Pet Trust or other arrangements to avoid probate for your other assets, your family is going to have to probate your estate anyway. You could then put a provision in your Will to provide additional funding for your Pet Trust.

Whether the majority of the property that funds your Revocable Pet Trust is set aside in your name as trustee while you are alive or whether the property passes into the Revocable Pet Trust through your Will, once the probate administration process is complete your Pet Trust will be funded with a sufficient amount of cash to provide for the care of your pet.

I'm tired after all of this planning. Can't we just sleep?

MANAGING THE PET TRUST PROPERTY.

The second duty of a trustee is to manage the trust property for the benefit of your pet. If you choose to fund your Pet Trust with cash, I suggest that you include a provision in your trust document requiring the Successor Trustee to keep the cash in an interest bearing account.

If you fund your Pet Trust with a complex portfolio of stocks, bonds and real estate, you need to choose a Successor Trustee who has the skills to manage the trust property for the benefit of your pet.

If the Pet Trust property is complex, you might want to consider a professional Successor Trustee.

PLEASE REMEMBER, WHILE YOU ARE ALIVE YOU CONTINUE TO MAKE ALL OF THE DECISIONS ABOUT THE PET TRUST PROPERTY.

 YOU ARE THE INITIAL TRUSTEE

 NOTHING CHANGES UNTIL YOU ARE GONE

WHEN DOES THE PET TRUST END?

In practical terms, the Pet Trust will end with the death of your pet or pets.

There are some fancy words that are included in the trust document to avoid the ancient concept of the "Rule Against Perpetuities", but you don't need to worry about that.

You need to be very careful to designate who will receive the remaining trust assets upon the death of your pet or pets. It's probably not a very good idea to name the physical caregiver as the person who will receive the remaining trust assets after the death of your pet. You want to be sure that your pet will be well cared for and there's no financial motivation for the caregiver to profit from the death of your pet.

There are no rules on who you name to receive the trust property after your pet's death.

Some people will name their family members as the ultimate takers and others will name a charity, most typically which benefits animals, to receive the trust assets after the death of your pet.

YOU HAVE NOW COMPLETED YOUR TRAINING ON HOW TO CREATE A REVOCABLE PET TRUST.

YOUR PETS WILL BE SO GRATEFUL!

Chapter Seven
WHAT IS A STATUTORY TRUST?
DO I WANT ONE FOR MY PET?

How does a Revocable Trust compare with a Statutory Trust?

A majority of the states have passed laws allowing what is known as a Statutory Trust. This type of trust does not require you, as the pet owner to make any decisions regarding the actual terms or provision of the trust.

The Statutory Pet Trust Law requires you to include a simple provision in your Will such as:

"I leave $5,000 in trust for the care of my pet."

The statutory pet law requires that the trust end when your pet dies. The Statutory Pet Trust Law allows for the appointment of a person to enforce the trust to make certain that the $5,000 is actually used for the care of your pet.

A Statutory Trust is really just a provision you include in your Will.

A person who is interested in your pet's welfare would need to go through all of the steps described in Chapter 4 before the money would be available. Then, there would be no instructions on how the money should be spent for your pet or pets.

It may be cheap to include a statutory trust in your Will, but expensive after you are gone.

It is wonderful and even critical that most of the states have passed a Statutory Pet Trust Law.

The Statutory Pet Trust Laws allow a person to include a very simple provision in his or her will that merely states,
"I leave XXX amount in trust for the benefit of my pet."

> It could be months before the Will is probated. What do I do until then?

But the really important part about the Statutory Pet Trust Laws is that before their enactment, YOU COULD NOT CREATE A TRUST FOR YOUR PET BECAUSE YOUR PET WAS NOT A PERSON.

PRIOR TO THE STATUTORY PET TRUST LAWS, A PET COULD NOT BE A BENEFICIARY.

Remember, with a Statutory Pet Trust provision in your Will, there is no money for your pet until the lengthy probate process is started and a Judge orders a distribution for your pet. This is not a very good idea.

Statutory Pet Trust Laws opened the book to allow for the creation of Revocable Pet Trusts!

If you are going to put provisions in your Will for your pet, I recommend that you include a **full trust** inside of your Will that contains all of the instructions and provisions I explained in Chapter Five.

This is called a Testamentary Trust. A Testamentary Trust 's provisions can be identical to the instructions you put in your Revocable Pet Trust. The difference is, you don't have to convey property to your Testamentary Trust because the Testamentary Trust is part of your Will and does not come into existence until you die.

HOW DO I CREATE A PET TRUST?

You have several options:

 You can finish reading this book and use the Pet Trust Form found in Chapter Nine. A user friendly key guides you through how to create a legally binding Pet Trust.

 You can contact me, Kimberly A. Colgate at kcolgate@FLLAWYER.com. I can create a custom plan for you and your pets.

 You can call my office at 941-927-2996. I will schedule a consultation with a pet planning lawyer.

You can contact your attorney. You might want to provide your attorney with a copy of this Book! Pet Trusts are new, and some attorneys might not be familiar with the new laws.

 You can go to **www.CreateAPetTrust.com** for more suggestions.

YOU BOUGHT THE BOOK! YOU ARE ALMOST DONE!

Chapter Eight
SPECIAL RULES FOR AN AMERICAN
KENNEL CLUB REGISTERED DOG

WHAT KIND OF PLAN DO YOU NEED?

The same decisions need to be made and planning techniques are available for an AKC registered dog. Namely, you can provide for your dog in your Will, which I did not recommend, or you can form a trust for the future care of your dog.

You need to follow all the recommended steps discussed in this book to prepare a plan for your dog.

IS THERE ANYTHING DIFFERENT FOR MY AKC REGISTERED DOG?

Yes. What is different about an AKC registered dog is that the American Kennel Club does not allow you to register ownership of your dog in the name of a trustee. This means that you cannot register your dog in your name as trustee, while you are alive, and, your AKC registered dog cannot be owned in the name of your Successor Trustee, after you are gone.

This presents a bit of a dilemma for our special Pet Trust Dog.

Don't worry, I'm going to explain your options.

Before you worry about what forms will be filed with the American Kennel Club, you need to make some fundamental decisions.

Planning for your dog in your Will. If you decide to transfer ownership of your dog in your Will, the new owner will need to register your dog in his or her name as part of the probate administration. I will explain how you can do that later in this chapter.

Creating a trust for your dog. You can still create a trust for the benefit of your dog, but one of the decisions you will need to make is who will be the AKC registered owner of your dog after you are gone.

WHAT DO YOU DO IF YOU WANT TO CREATE A TRUST FOR YOUR AKC REGISTERED DOG?

You can still create a trust for your dog, but you will need to decide whether your dog will be registered in in the name of the Physical Caregiver, or, the Successor Trustee can register your dog in his or her individual name, and not in his or her name as Successor Trustee, or you can designate that the dog be registered with the AKC in the name of an independent third person.

There is no perfect answer.

Option One: Your Physical Caregiver will own and register your dog with the AKC.

If your physical caregiver owns your dog after you are gone, it may be more difficult to get him or her to transfer ownership to another physical caregiver if for some reason the physical caregiver is no longer able to serve. Your physical caregiver may not be able to continue to serve for a myriad of reasons.

Perhaps the physical caregiver can no longer care for your dog due to changed circumstances. Or, what if the unthinkable happens, and your physical caregiver is either not providing for your pet according to the instructions in your trust document, or your physical caregiver dies.

Option Two: The Successor Trustee you name in your Pet Trust will register your dog with the AKC in his or her individual name.

You could have your Successor Trustee become the new owner of your AKC registered dog. Your Successor Trustee would have to register to take title in his or her individual name, because the American Kennel Club does not allow ownership in the name of a trustee.

Unless there is some compelling reason to have your physical caregiver own your AKC registered dog, it is probably a better idea to have your dog owned and registered in the individual name of your Successor Trustee. This will allow your Successor Trustee to make all of the legal decisions about your dog and maintain more control and insure that the instructions in your trust document are being followed.

Option Three: You can instruct that your dog will be owned and registered by an independent third party, like your breeder.

This might be a good alternative for a professional breeder. Your fellow breeder may be more likely to understand the professional development of your dog. Often a fellow breeder might not be able to act as the Successor Trustee, or become the physical caregiver of your dog, but your fellow breeder would be the AKC registered owner who would sign show entries, make breeding decisions and sign any legal documents associated with your dog or your dog's puppies.

WHICH FORMS NEED TO BE FILED WITH THE AMERICAN KENNEL CLUB?

The American Kennel Club does not allow reproduction of their forms. I recommend you go to:

www.akc.org   On the left, you will see a choice "Downloadable Forms" Click on the Downloadable Forms. You will need to print two forms:

First Form: Statement of Legal Rights
Second Form: Supplemental Transfer Statement

Both forms will be needed to register your dog with its new owner after you are gone. After you have printed these two forms, it will be easier to understand the explanation of how to use them.

Statement of Legal Rights Form

The Statement of Legal Rights Form must be filed with the AKC to give the Executor named in your Will, or if there is no Will, your Next of Kin, the power to transfer ownership of your AKC registered dog.

When you print the form from www.akc.org, you will see that the form asks the Executor of your Will or, if there is no Executor, then the next of kin to fill in the name, address and date of death of the former owner.

Then, the Statement of Legal Rights Form asks that either the Executor or the next of kin provide the name, address and telephone number of the person who will sign a Supplemental Transfer Statement Form. The Supplemental Transfer Statement is the form that is filed with the AKC to actually change the owner of your AKC registered dog. The Statement of Legal Rights Form is the form that your Executor or next of kin files with the AKC first, to give permission or power for the named person to change the registration and convey title to a new owner.

The Executor, if there is a Will, or the next of kin, if there is no Will, must sign the Statement of Legal Rights Form in the presence of a notary, and mail the form to the AKC.

If the Statement of Legal Rights is being completed by your Executor, he or she must attach the Letters of Administation or the Letters of Authority [as they are known in some states] to the Statement of Legal Rights Form. If there is no probate proceeding, and no Executor has been appointed, the next of kin may sign and submit the Statement of Legal Rights, without attaching Letters of Administration.

NOTICE, THIS FORM DOES NOT ACTUALLY TRANSFER OWNERSHIP OF YOUR DOG!

The form only authorized the Executor or your next of kin to complete the Supplemental Transfer Form.

Supplemental Transfer Form

The Supplemental Transfer Form is used anytime your dog has been transfered more than once before applying for registration in the name of the current owner. If you are alive and you want to transfer ownership to another individual, you would use the Supplemental Transfer Form to change the AKC registration and ownership of your dog to a new owner.

The Supplemental Transfer Form is also used to change registration and ownership after the dog owner dies. After you are gone, and after your Executor or next of kin has filed the Statement of Legal Rights Form with the AKC, your Executor or next of kin will then prepare and file the Supplemental Transfer Form to transfer the registration to the new owner. Remember, the new owner will either be someone you name in your Will or the new owner will be the Successor Trustee, the Physical Caregiver or an independent third person.

The Executor or next of kin uses the Supplemental Transfer Form to identify the dog or dog that is being transferred, and to register the new owner.

Your Executor or next of kin will need to attach a copy of your dog's AKC Registration Certificate to the Supplemental Transfer Statement.

I RECOMMEND THAT YOU FIND YOUR DOG'S AKC REGISTRATION CERTIFICATE AND PUT IT IN YOUR PET PLAN AND PET TRUST BOOK!

If your Executor cannot find your dog's AKC Reistration Certificate, your Executor or next of kin can contact the AKC to order a duplicate form.

HOW DO YOU USE THE STATEMENT OF LEGAL RIGHTS FORM AND THE SUPPLEMENTAL TRANSFER FORM?

Option One: You are NOT going to create a trust for your dog, but you have a Will.

If you have a Will, you either included instructions in your Will for your dog, or, you have a Will but it does not mention your dog.

If your Will does not mention your dog, your family or friends will have to decide who will take your dog. I'M SURE THAT WON'T HAPPEN AFTER YOU READ THIS BOOK!

Because you have a Will, your Executor will be the only person who is authorized to change the registration of your AKC dog and transfer ownership to the new owner.

Your Executor will need to:

1. Complete a Statement of Legal Rights Form and attach a copy of the Letters of Administration or the Letters of Authority issued by the local Probate Court. The completed form and a copy of the Letters of Administration must be sent to the AKC before the AKC will allow your Executor to transfer ownership of your dog.

2. After the Executor files the Statement of Legal Rights, he or she may complete the Supplemental Transfer Statement. This is the document that actually changes the registration and ownership to the new owner.

Remember, you must attach a copy of your dog's AKC Registration Certificate with the Supplemental Transfer Statement.

It doesn't matter whether or not your Will names a new owner for your dog. If you have a Will, your Executor is the only person who can transfer ownership of your dog after you are gone. The Executor must still file both a Statement of Legal Rights Form and a Supplemental Transfer Statement with the AKC in order to register your dog to its new owner. If you have included instructions in your Will for your dog, your Executor knows who to name as the new owner. If your Will contains no instructions regarding your dog, the Executor is still the one who must complete the Statement of Legal Rights Form and the Supplemental Transfer Form to transfer the registration to the new owner.

Even if you don't create a trust for your dog, you should still include a provision in your Will directing who will receive your dog after you are gone. If you don't put instructions in your Will about who will own your dog after you are gone, your Executor is going to have to guess what you would have wanted.

What if you have made no provision for your dog in your Will or there is no probate administration? If there is no probate administration, then no Executor is appointed. The AKC rules allow your next of kin to complete both the Statement of Legal Rights Form and the Supplemental Transfer Form to register the new owner of your dog with the AKC. Your heirs or next of kin now have the same problem. They may not know who you would have wanted to own your dog after you are gone.

If you want to understand why your next of kin may not need to open a probate administration and why there will be no Executor appointed, call my office at 941-927-2997. You can order my book, **The Everything Wills & Estate Planning Book.** It teaches you all about probate administration, Executors and what you need to do to create an estate plan for you that will avoid probate administration for your family.

Recommendation: If you have a Will and your Will has named an Executor, why don't you print the Statement of Legal Rights form from www.akc.org and complete the form naming your Executor as the one authorized to register and transfer title to your AKC dog after you are gone.

Don't sign the form! Your Executor will need to sign the Statement of Legal Rights Form after you are gone. But, this is one more thing you can do for the future of your dog.

Also, print and complete the Supplemental Transfer Statement. Don't sign the Form! Your Executor or next of kin and the new owner will sign the Supplemental Transfer Statement after you are gone.

Put both forms in your book, along with a copy of your dog's AKC Registration Certificate.

Option Two: You are going to create a Pet Trust for your dog.

If you decide to provide for the care of your dog in a Pet Trust, there are a few more choices you will need to make.

The American Kennel Club rules do not allow a dog to be registered in the name of a Trustee. Therefore, you are going to have to decide whether you want your Successor Trustee to own your dog in his or her individual name, whether the Physical Caregiver is going to own your dog or whether you are going to name an independent person. Namely, you are going to name someone that is not related to the trust as the new owner.

What forms will be needed and who will sign them?

The AKC still requires a Statement of Legal Rights Form and a Supplemental Transfer Form to be filed with the AKC in order to change the registration and ownership of your dog.

The AKC does not recognize a Trustee as having authority to sign these forms. Therefore, even if you have created a trust for your dog, either your Executor, if you have a Will or your next of kin, if you have no Will, must complete both the Statement of Legal Rights Form and the Supplemental Transfer Form.

If you want to be absolutely certain that your dog is owned by the right people, you should have a provision in your Will which names the future owner of your AKC registered dog. That new owner, would be either the Successor Trustee, the Physical Caregiver or a Third Person.

The trust will still provide all of the support for your dog, but the instructions on who will own and register your AKC dog should be included in your Will.

If you don't have a Will, you should leave written instructions for your next of kin on how to complete the Statement of Legal Rights Form and the Supplemental Transfer Form.

Again, it would be alot easier if you print and complete both the Legal Rights Form and the Supplemental Transfer Form and put it in your Pet Plan and Pet Trust Book.

CAN YOU FILE THESE FORMS WITH THE AKC BEFORE YOU DIE?

No! The Statement of Legal Rights Form can only be signed by your Executor or your next of kin. I don't mean to be indelicate, but you need to be dead in order to have an Executor or a next of kin.

You can complete the form, include it in your book and have it ready to be signed. But, it cannot be filed until after you are gone.

You could elect to transfer ownership of your AKC Registered Dog before you die. Then, you would be completing and filing the Supplemental Transfer Form while you are alive and naming a new owner. Let's face it, most people are not going to register and transfer ownership of their AKC dog while they are alive just to make sure someone owns the dog after they are gone.

But, you might consider co-ownership. You can co-own your AKC Registered Dog with the person whom you want to own the dog after you are gone. Then, if you die, the co-owner, as the survivor, automatically continues to own the dog, with no further AKC filings.

I recommend that you print the Statement of Legal Rights and the Supplemental Transfer Form while you are alive. Fill it out and put it in your Pet Plan and Pet Trust Guide Book. Then, the next of kin only needs to sign the forms and submit them to the American Kennel Club.

ISN'T THERE AN EASIER WAY? MY FRIEND TOLD ME I COULD JUST COMPLETE A POWER OF ATTORNEY FORM.

This advice could not be MORE INCORRECT!

WHAT IS A POWER OF ATTORNEY FORM?

The AKC provides a Power of Attorney Form on their website at www.akc.org. This form allows you to appoint a person whom you authorize and the AKC will recognize as having the power to transfer AKC ownership of your dog. There are several very significant issues associated with this form.

🐾 First. A Power of Attorney Form **cannot** be used if you are deceased. In the legal perspective, all powers of attorney die with you.

The AKC Power of Attorney Form cannot be used by your Executor, Personal Representative, Heirs or Successor Trustee to transfer ownership of your AKC dog after you are gone.

🐾 Second. The Power of Attorney Form must be renewed or refiled with the AKC every year. Therefore, the Power of Attorney Form really is only meant for you, as the dog owner, to give another person temporary (1 year) power to register your dog in another person's name, WHILE YOU ARE LIVING.

🐾 Third, the AKC Power of Attorney Form cannot be used to transfer ownership of your AKC registered dog if you are incapacitated. The AKC Power of Attorney Form is not the type of power of attorney that can be used unless you, the dog owner, are competent.

That is why there is a special Incapacitated Authorization Form which will allow your named agent to be able to convey title, should you become incapacitated.

As you can see, the Power of Attorney Form has a very limited use and CANNOT BE USED TO TRANSFER OWNERSHIP OF YOUR DOG AFTER YOU ARE GONE!

INCAPACITATED AUTHORIZATION FORM

An Incapacitated Authorization Form allows you to appoint a person as your agent, who is authorized to transfer ownership of your AKC registered dog, should you become incapacitated.

Under what circumstances would you use this form?

Many people, as part of their own estate plan will execute a Durable Power of Attorney. This is a special power of attorney where you, the grantor, appoint a person, known as the agent, who can sign any legal or financial documents, in the event of your incapacity. Unlike the AKC Power of Attorney Form, the agent you appoint with a Durable Power of Attorney can sign legal documents after you become incapacitated.

If you have a Durable Power of Attorney appointing an agent to act for you if you become incapacitated, one of the powers your agent has is to transfer title to any property you own, including your dog.

While you are competent, you can have your estate planning lawyer prepare a Durable Power of Attorney For you.

Then, you can complete and file the Incapacitation Authorization Notice with the American Kennel Club, along with a copy of your Durable Power of Attorney. When you file the Incapacitated Authorization Notice with the American Kennel Club, you are in essence pre-registering with the American Kennel Club and giving your agent the power to convey or transfer title to your AKC registered dog should you become incapacitated.

As part of your emergency pet plan, hopefully you have decided who would take your dog in the event you become incapacitated and are no longer able to care for your dog. Filing this form merely gives your agent the power to carry out your instructions.

SUMMARY

As you can see, whether you decide to provide for the long-term care of you dog in your Will or whether you decide to create a Pet Trust, your Executor or your next of kin will need to sign and file a Statement of Legal Rights Form and a Supplemental Transfer Statement Form with the AKC to transfer the registration and ownership of your dog.

You now understand the forms that will need to be filed with the American Kennel Club to make your plan happen.

I'm sure glad all that complicated paperwork is done. I'd hate to be owned by no one!

Congratulations!

You have learned the rules and you are now ready to create your Revocable Pet Trust. Pages 168-173 gives you a key to completing your Revocable Pet Trust. For each numbered key, turn to pages 168-173 for instructions on how to complete your Revocable Pet Trust. You can write the information in the book.

When you complete your Revocable Pet Trust, you will need to sign the document in the book in the presence of two witnesses and a notary.

Chapter Nine
REVOCABLE PET TRUST

[1]_____ REVOCABLE PET TRUST

I, [2]_____, a resident of
[3]_____ do hereby enter into the [1]_____
_____ REVOCABLE PET TRUST between myself as
Settlor and myself as Trustee.

WITNESSETH:
ARTICLE I
ESTABLISHMENT OF TRUST

1.1 Name of Trust. This Trust may be referred to as the [1]_____
_____ REVOCABLE PET TRUST.

1.2 Declarations.   I have [4]_____ pets: [5]_____

_____

_____

My pets identified in this Article shall hereinafter be referred to as "my pets."

1.3 Trust Corpus. I hereby transfer and deliver $1 Dollar to myself as Trustee. All trust property shall be held by the Trustee in trust as is provided in this Agreement.

1.4 Additional Trust Property. From time to time I or any other person(s) may individually or jointly transfer additional property to this Trust or to any separate trust established hereunder. Additions of property may be made from any source by assignment, conveyance or delivery, or by any testamentary disposition or appointment. Additions of life insurance policy proceeds or other monies payable on death may be made by designation of the Trustee as a beneficiary thereof.

ARTICLE II
RESERVATIONS

2.1 Amendment and Revocation.   I may, during my lifetime and without the consent of anyone, revoke this Agreement in whole or in part (whereupon the trust property or the part affected by such revocation shall be distributed in accordance with my instructions) or amend it from time to time in any respect, except that the duties and compensation of the Trustee shall not be materially changed by any amendment without the Trustee's written approval.

ARTICLE III
LIFETIME MANAGEMENT

3.1 Income.   The Trustee shall pay to me the net income, if any, in such installments and amounts as I direct. In the absence of such direction, net income not distributed shall be accumulated and become part of the principal.

3.2 Invasion of Principal.   The Trustee shall have the discretionary power to pay me such principal as will, when combined with my other income, support and maintain me so that I might, as near as possible with due regard to my total estate and my future financial requirements for myself and my dependents known to the Trustee, continue to enjoy the standard of living to which I am accustomed.

This power shall be liberally construed without regard to remaindermen's interests and shall also include amounts for the care, support, education, medical and dental care, and general welfare and well being of persons dependent on me, premiums on life insurance on my life whether or not such policies are assigned to or payable to the Trustee, and all sums necessary to preserve and protect my property.

ARTICLE IV
CONSEQUENCES OF DEATH

4.1 Death.   At my death this Agreement shall be irrevocable. The Trustee shall receive and hold as part of this Trust all then remaining principal and undistributed net income. After my death the Trustee shall administer and distribute this Trust in accordance with the provisions of Article V.

ARTICLE V
DURATION AND DISTRIBUTION OF TRUST

5.1 Rest and Remainder of Accumulated Income and Principal Shall Be Used For The Support Of My Pets Identified in Article 1.2. The rest and remainder of the accumulated income and principal shall be held in trust for the benefit of my pets. My Successor Trustee shall administer the accumulated income and principal as follows:

(1) Caregivers. I hereby appoint [6]_____as the Physical Caregiver of my pets. If [6]_____ cannot serve, I appoint [7]_____ as Physical Caregiver. If [6]_____ and [7]_____ are not able to serve, they shall appoint a successor Physical Caregiver. If either [6]_____ or [7]_____ are not available to appoint a successor Physical Caregiver, the survivor shall appoint a successor Physical Caregiver. If both [6]_____ and [7]_____ are not available to serve and are not available to appoint a successor Physical Caregiver, my Successor Trustee shall appoint a Physical Caregiver.

(2) Instructions For The Care of My Pets. My Physical Caregiver shall be required to provide the following care for my pets:

[8]_____

_____

_____

_____

_____

_____

_____

_____

_____

_____

_____

_____

_____

_____

_____

_____

(3) Payments To Be Made By My Successor Trustee.

[9]

It is my intention that all of the income and principal of the trust could be used for the care of my pets without regard to the remainderman's interest.

The primary purpose of this trust is to provide for the care and comfort of my pets. If my Successor Trustee determines, in his or her sole discretion, that the Physical Caregiver is not providing my pets with the proper care and comfort, or is not following the instructions contained in this document, I hereby give my Successor Trustee the power to remove my pets from the Physical Caregiver's home, and appoint a new Physical Caregiver.

Any person, other than the Successor Trustee, who feels that my pets are not receiving the care and comfort I have provided for, shall have standing to petition the court to remove the trustee or caregivers.

5.2 Distribution of the Remaining Accumulated Income and Principal After The Death of [5] _____.

After the death of my pets have been confirmed to my Successor Trustee, the accumulated income and principal of the trust shall be paid as follows:

[10]_____

_____

_____

_____

_____

_____

_____

_____

_____

_____

_____

_____

_____

_____

ARTICLE VI
TRUSTEE

6.1 Trustee. Any trustee shall have the right to resign at any time by giving ninety (90) days notice to the Successor Trustee. I hereby appoint myself, [2]_____, as Trustee. If I am not living or I am disabled and not capable of serving as trustee, I hereby appoint [11]_____as Successor Trustee. If [11]_____ is not available to serve, I hereby appoint [12]_____.

6.2 Fees. The Successor Trustee shall be compensated [13]_____ Dollars per year for serving as Successor Trustee. The Successor Trustee shall also be reimbursed for all expenses and charges incurred in the performance of its duties or by reason of its office as Successor Trustee.

6.3 Disabled Trustee.   A Trustee is "disabled" (and while disabled shall not serve as Trustee) if the next Successor Trustee receives written certification that the examined Trustee is physically or mentally incapable of managing the affairs of the trust, whether or not there is an adjudication of the Trustee's incompetence.

6.3(a) Certification of Disability.   This certification shall be valid only if it is signed by at least two (2) physicians, each of whom has personally examined the Trustee and at least one (1) of whom is board certified in the specialty most closely associated with the alleged disability. This certification need not indicate any cause for the Trustee's disability. A certification of disability shall be rescinded when a serving Trustee receives a certification the former Trustee is capable of managing the trust's affairs. This certification, too, shall be valid only if it is signed by at least two (2) physicians, each of whom has personally examined the Trustee and at least one (1) of whom is board certified in the specialty most closely associated with the former disability.

6.3(b) Reliance on Certification.   No person is liable to anyone for actions taken in reliance on the certification under this paragraph, or for dealing with a Trustee other than the one removed for disability based on these certifications.

ARTICLE VII
POWERS OF TRUSTEE AND OTHER PROVISIONS

7.1 Powers of Trustee While I, [2]_____**, am serving as Trustee.** While I, [2]_____, am serving as Trustee, I shall have full and complete authority to make any decisions on behalf of the trust that I could have made, had I owned the trust property in my individual name. Those powers shall include, but not be limited to the power to:

    (a) To receive and retain the initial Trust corpus and all other property which I may hereafter transfer to the Trustee either during my lifetime, by Will or other testamentary disposition, or which any other person may hereafter transfer to the Trustee, the Trustee shall receive all such property as part of the Trust even though it may not be a legal investment for the Trustee and even though such property by reason of its character may not be an appropriate trust investment apart from this provision. The Trustee is authorized to retain its own stock or other securities or stock or securities of any affiliate or holding company, which owns the Trustee.

(b) To sell, exchange, give options upon, partition or otherwise dispose of any property which the Trustee may hold from time to time, at public or private sale, or otherwise, for cash or other consideration or on credit, and upon such terms and for such consideration as the Trustee deems advisable; and to transfer and convey such property free of all trust.

(c) To invest and reinvest in any property, real or personal, including (without limiting the generality of the foregoing language) securities of domestic and foreign corporations and investment trusts, bonds, preferred stocks, common stocks, option contracts, "short sales", mortgages and mortgage participations, even though such investment by reason of its character, amount, proportion to the total trust estate or otherwise would not be considered appropriate for a fiduciary apart from this provision, and even though such investment causes a greater proportion of the total trust to be invested in investments of one type or of one company than would be considered appropriate for a fiduciary apart from this provision. Such investment may be on a cash or margin basis, and the Trustee, for such purpose, may maintain and operate cash or margin accounts with brokers, and may deliver and pledge securities held or purchased by the Trustee with such brokers both as security for loans and advances made to the Trustee and to insure the ability of the Trustee to deliver stock against short options.

In addition, the Trustee may purchase life insurance even though it is non income-producing. The Trustee is authorized to invest in any common fund, legal or discretionary, which may be operated by and/or under the control of a corporate Trustee.

(d) To make loans, secured or unsecured, in such amounts, upon such terms, at such rates of interest, and to such persons, trusts, corporations or other parties as the Trustee deems advisable.

(e) To improve real estate, including the power to demolish buildings in whole or in part and to erect new buildings; to lease (including leasing for oil, gas and minerals) real estate on such terms as the Trustee deems advisable, including the power to give leases for periods that extend beyond the duration of any trust; to foreclose, extend, assign, partially release and discharge mortgages.

(f) To collect, pay, contest, compromise or abandon, upon such terms and evidence as the Trustee deems advisable, any claims, including taxes, either in favor of or against trust property or the Trustee; to abandon or surrender any property.

(g) To employ brokers, banks, custodians, investment counsel, attorneys, accountants and other agents, and to delegate to them such duties, rights and powers of the Trustee (including the right to vote shares of stock held by the Trustee) for such periods as the Trustee deems advisable.

(h) To hold and register securities in the name of a nominee with or without the addition of words indicating such securities are held in a fiduciary capacity; to hold and register securities in a securities depository or in any other form convenient for the Trustee.

(i) To participate in any voting trust, merger, reorganization, consolidation or liquidation affecting trust property and, in connection therewith, to deposit any trust property with or under the direction of any protective committee and to exchange any trust property for other property.

(j) To exercise any stock or other kind of option.

(k) To keep trust property in [14] _____ or elsewhere, or with a depository or custodian.

(l) To determine (reasonably and in accordance with sound trust accounting principles) as to all sums of money or other things of value received by the Trustee, whether and to what extent the same shall be deemed to be principal or to be income, and as to all charges or expenses paid by the Trustee, whether and to what extent the same shall be charged against principal or against income, including the power to apportion any receipt or expense between principal and income and to determine what part, if any, of the actual income received upon any wasting investment or upon any security purchased or acquired at a premium shall be retained and added to principal to prevent a diminution of principal upon exhaustion or maturity thereof. The Trustee may also establish reserves for depreciation and anticipated expenses and fund such reserves for depreciation and anticipated expenses with appropriate charges against income. All determinations made pursuant to this subparagraph by the Trustee shall be made fairly to balance the interest of the income beneficiary and the remaindermen. The Trustee shall resolve all doubtful questions in favor of the income beneficiary. If an income beneficiary also serves as one of the Trustees of the Trust, then the income beneficiary-Trustee shall not exercise any of the powers granted by this subparagraph and all such powers shall be exercised by the other Trustee(s) only.

(m) To distribute the trust estate in cash or in kind, or partly in cash and partly in kind, as the Trustee deems advisable, and for purposes of distribution, to value the assets reasonably and in good faith as of the date of distribution. Such valuation shall be conclusive on all beneficiaries. The Trustee shall not be required to distribute a proportionate amount of each asset to each beneficiary but may instead make non pro-rata distributions. In making distribution, the Trustee may, but shall not be required to, take account of the income tax basis in relation to market value of assets distrib-uted. Distribution may be made directly to the beneficiary, to a legally-appointed Guardian or Conservator or, where permitted by law, to a custodian under any Uniform Gifts to Minors Act, including a custodian selected by the Trustee.

If you don't plan it...it just won't happen.

(n) To deposit monies to be paid to a beneficiary who is a minor in any demand, savings bank or savings and loan account maintained in the sole name of the minor and to accept the deposit receipt as a full acquittance.

(o) To accept the receipt of a minor as a full acquittance.

(p) To borrow from anyone (including the Trustee or any affiliate) in the name of the Trust, to execute promissory notes therefore and to secure obligations by mortgage or pledge of trust property, provided the Trustee shall not be personally liable and that any such loan shall be payable out of trust assets only.

(q) To hold, manage, invest and account for any separate trust in one or more consolidated funds, in whole or in part, as the Trustee deems advisable. As to each consolidated fund, the division into the various shares comprising such fund need to be made only on the Trustee's books of account, in which each separate trust shall be allocated its proportionate share of principal and income of the fund and charged with its proportionate share of the expenses. No such holding shall defer any distribution.

(r) To carry, at the expense of the Trust, insurance of such kinds and in such amounts as the Trustee deems advisable to protect the trust estate and the Trustee personally against any hazard or liability.

(s) To exercise all of these powers without application to any court.

7.2 Powers of Successor Trustee After the Death or Disability of [2]_____.

After my death or disability, the financial powers of the Successor Trustee shall be substantially restricted. The primary purpose of this trust, after my death or disability, is to provide for the care and comfort of my pets. After my death or disability, my Successor Trustee shall:

(a)   Liquidate all trust assets to cash, within thirty (30) days of my death or disability. If my trust owns assets not capable of liquidation within thirty (30) days of my death or disability, my Successor Trustee shall take all reasonably necessary steps to sell these assets.

(b)   Invest the cash received upon liquidation or sale of the trust property in a liquid money market, or Certificates of Deposit.

(c)   My Successor Trustee is not authorized, after my death or disability, to invest in any trust assets other than cash, cash accounts, certificates of deposits, or other cash equivalents.

(d)   My Successor Trustee shall have the legal standing and power to take any action necessary to enforce the provisions of this trust for the benefit of my pets.

(e)   My Trustee is directed to invest the trust property as herein specified, without regard to the remainderman's interest.

7.3   Diversification. The Trustee shall not be required to diversify assets and shall invest the trust corpus according to the instructions contained in this document.

7.4   Construction. This Agreement, all trusts established hereunder, and all other matters shall be constructed under and regulated by [14]_____ law. The validity of this Agreement and all trusts established hereunder shall be determined by [14]_____ law.

7.5 Certificate of Trust Existence and Authority. The Trustee may at any time record, file or deliver a Certificate of Trust Existence and Authority with or to any clerk, register of deeds, transfer agent or other similar agency or office or to any person dealing with the Trustee. Such Certificate shall contain a verbatim synopsis of certain provisions of this Agreement and shall be signed and acknowledged by the Trustee. Any purchaser or person dealing with the Trustee shall be entitled to rely on such Certificate as a full state-ment of the provisions of this Agreement which are pertinent to the particu-lar transaction. Machine copies of the executed Certificate shall have the same effect and authority as the executed Certificate.

ARTICLE VIII
ACCOUNTING & EXCULPATORY CLAUSE

My Successor Trustee shall not be required to prepare an annual accounting. My Successor Trustee shall prepare an annual tax return, if necessary. After the death of my pets, my Successor Trustee shall make the last three (3) years of bank statements and tax returns available for the review of the remainder-men, in lieu of an accounting.

My Successor Trustee shall not be liable to the remainderman for any reason, unless my Successor Trustee has committed fraud or has otherwise intentionally damaged the interest of the remaindermen.

The books and records of the Successor Trustee relating to duties as Successor Trustee of this Trust shall be open during business hours for inspection by me or any beneficiary of this Trust or their duly-appointed attorney, accountant, agent or other representative.

IN WITNESS WHEREOF, I have hereunto set my hand and seal as of this _____ day of _____, 200_.

Signed in the presence of:

_____   _____

- Witness   [2]
                                         Settlor/Trustee

_____

-Witness

STATE OF _____)

) ss

COUNTY OF _____)

On this _____ day of _____, 200_, before me personally appeared [2]_____, who being duly sworn, says that he or she has read the foregoing TRUST AGREEMENT by him or her signed as Settlor and Trustee, and he or she knows the contents thereof and agrees to the conditions and terms therein.

_____

Notary Public

My Commission Expires:

KEY TO COMPLETING YOUR PET TRUST

1. Insert the name of the trust. I recommend using your full name.
        For example, KIMBERLY A. COLGATE REVOCABLE PET TRUST.
2. Insert your name.
3. Insert the city and state of your residence.
4. Insert the number of pets who will benefit from this trust.
5. Insert the name and breed of your pets.
6. Insert the name of the person you are naming as your first choice for
    the Physical Caregiver of your pets.
7. Insert the name of the person who will serve as Physical Caregiver, if
    your first choice is not available to serve, or declines to serve.
8. Insert the instructions and duties to be performed by the Physical
        Caregiver of your pets. I have provided you with plenty of space to
        write the instructions and duties in the book.

Here are samples of instructions and duties you might consider including in your Pet Trust:

a.   My caregiver must reside in a house with a backyard that has grass and is entirely fenced.

b.   My caregiver must take my pets to a licensed veterinarian, no less frequently than annually.

c.   My caregiver must seek any necessary veterinarian care for my pets.

d.   My caregiver must provide a neat, clean, peaceful and habitable environment in the house for my pets.

e.   My caregiver must allow my Successor Trustee to inspect the premises with or without notice.

f.   My caregiver must provide my Successor Trustee with documentation, on an annual basis, to establish that they have provided the care outlined herein for my pets.

THESE ARE JUST SAMPLES. YOU CAN INCLUDE ANY INSTRUCTIONS YOU WANT THE PHYSICAL CAREGIVER TO FOLLOW.

9.   Insert the payments your Successor Trustee must make to the Physical Caregiver for the care of your pet. It will help to develop a budget for the care of your pets. Chapter 5 gave you a sample budget. This will help you define both the required and discretionary payments your Physical Caregiver must make for the benefit of your pets.

Here are samples of payments you might consider requiring your Successor Trustee to make for the benefit of your pets:

    a.   My Successor Trustee shall make an initial payment to my Physical Caregiver to pay for any improvements or costs incurred to prepare the Physical Caregiver's home for my pets. My Physical Caregiver must submit a budget to my Successor Trustee and confirm the expenditures with the production of receipts. My Successor Trustee may pay my Physical Caregiver up to Three Thousand ($3,000) Dollars for the initial start-up expenditures.
    b.   My Successor Trustee shall pay the Physical Caregiver compensation in the amount of $6,000.00 per year. The payment shall be made annually, at the beginning of the year, commencing within thirty (30) days of my death.

c. My Successor Trustee shall distribute Three Hundred ($300.00) Dollars per month to the Physical Caregiver for the routine expenses associated with the care of my pets. The first monthly payment shall be made within thirty (30) days of my death. This distribution is meant to compensate the Physical Caregivers for the cost of food, toys and miscellaneous items.

d. In addition to the payments specified in paragraph (c), my Successor Trustee shall pay all veterinarian bills incurred for the care of my pets.

e. My Successor Trustee must distribute such other amounts of income or principal as the Successor Trustee deems is necessary for the care and comfort of my pets.

f. My pets shall never be left in a commercial kennel during the Physical Caregiver's absence. If the Physical Caregiver is not available, I hereby instruct my Successor Trustee to pay for a pet sitter to come to my caregiver's house to stay with my pets. The only circumstances under which my pets shall remain or be placed in a kennel, is for medical treatment.

10. Insert the instructions regarding who is to receive the trust assets after your pets are gone.

11. Insert the name of the person who will serve as Successor Trustee after you are gone.

12. Insert the name of a person who will serve as Successor Trustee if your first choice is not available.

13. Insert the amount of compensation your Successor Trustee shall receive.

14. Insert the name of your state of residence.

You can fill in the Pet Trust Document Form using the Create A Pet Trust Form and Key.

If you prepare your Pet Trust Document by filling in the blanks, MAKE SURE YOU TAKE THE BOOK AND SIGN YOUR NAME IN THE PRESENCE OF TWO WITNESSES AND A NOTARY.

If you do not want to use the form provided the The Pet Plan and Pet Trust Guide Book, you can contact our pet specialists at 941-927-2996.

We can create a customized Pet Trust for your pets.

Please visit our web site at:
www.CreateAPetTrust.COM

175

About the Author

Kimberly A. Colgate graduated from law school in 1979. She enjoyed the distinction of graduating number one in her law school class out of 165 students. She continued her education and earned her Masters In Taxation. From 1983 – 1997 she was a full time Law Professor teaching Wills & Trusts, Federal Income Taxation and Estate Planning. During her tenure as a Law Professor she had the opportunity to author hundreds of papers and to lecture on Wills & Trusts across the country.

Kimberly left full time teaching in 1997 and opened a private law practice in Sarasota, Florida. While practicing law full time, Kimberly authored The Everything Wills & Estate Planning Book, which is sold in every major bookstore.

Kimberly A. Colgate brings 30 years of experience as a scholar, an author and a practicing attorney to teach you how to create a legal plan for your pets. Her collaboration with California illustrator Debby Carman will make you laugh, giggle and maybe even cry, while you learn the rules on how to create a legal plan for your pet.

About the Illustrator

Debby Carman is a renown Laguna Beach, California artist, children's book author and illustrator, cartoonist and ceramicist.

Debby has a fine art gallery in Laguna Beach featuring her distinctive style of art, sculpture, and her ceramic creations and paintings. Her manufacturing company, Faux Paw Productions produces the world's most beautiful ceramic pet bowls, known the world over.

Faux Paw Productions has a book publishing division as well as Faux Paw Media group which is currently co producing an animated preschool television series for broadcast and it's first full length feature film based on Debby's books and characters.

Emperically self taught, Debby creates "characters and art with heart, because everybody smiles in the same language." She lives in a tiny house by the sparkling sea with her dog Paddy Tickles and two 30+ lbs cats, Sunny Cheesepuss and Biggy Smalls.

Contact Debby direct @ 949-233-2082, email @ debbycarman@cox.net
Or visit the Faux Paw Productions website @ www.fauxpawproductions.com

Please cut card out and place in your wallet

In Case of Emergency

The holder of this card has a PET at home that will need attending to in the event of an emergency.

Pet Owner(s) Name _____

Pet Owner(s) Address _____

_____

Pet Owner(s) Home Phone Number _____

My Pet will need Attention. Please call my designated pet caregiver at

_____

Caregiver's Name _____

The Pet Plan and Pet Trust Guide

Pet Identification Card

Pet's Name _____ Male ____ Female ____

Breed _____ Birthdate or Age _____

Color _____ Weight _____

Pet License # _____ Microchip # _____

All details concerning this pet can be located in My "Pet Plan and Pet Trust Guide" Book located at _____

_____